Memories of You

Memories of You

Wendy Lill

Talonbooks
2003

Talonbooks
P.O. Box 2076, Vancouver, British Columbia, Canada V6B 3S3
www.talonbooks.com

Typeset in New Baskerville and printed and bound in Canada.

First Printing: December 2003

National Library of Canada Cataloguing in Publication Data
Lill, Wendy, 1950–
Memories of you / Wendy Lill.
A play.
ISBN 0-88922-489-7

1. Smart, Elizabeth, 1913–1986 —Drama. I. Title.
PS8573.I429M45 2003   C812'.54   C2003-910959-3

The publisher gratefully acknowledges the financial support of the
Canada Council for the Arts; the Government of Canada through the
Book Publishing Industry Development Program; and the Province of
British Columbia through the British Columbia Arts Council for our
publishing activities.

For my sons,
Samuel and Joseph

Memories of You premiered September 20, 1988, at the Prairie Theatre Exchange, Winnipeg, Manitoba with the following cast:

ELIZABETH: ....Joy Coghill
ROSE: ....Cheryl Swarts
BETTY: ....Karen Barker
LOUISE: ....Evelyne Anderson
GEORGE: ....Tom McBeath

Director: Kim McCaw
Set and costume design: Gwen Keatley
Lighting design: Larry Isacoff
Stage Manager: Janet Remy
Assistant Director: Maggie Nagle

Characters

ELIZABETH
ROSE
BETTY, the young ELIZABETH
LOUISE, BETTY's mother
GEORGE

The Setting

The set must allow for these various locales:
— the kitchen living area of a country cottage, Suffolk, England
— a garden
— a debutante's bedroom
— a summerhouse, California
— a cramped flat in wartime London
— a book launching
— a more upscale flat, London.

Because the play is about memory, both the sets and the scenes have the unfinished floating qualities of memories.

Act One

The kitchen living area of a country cottage. Suffolk,
England. ROSE, 25, is sitting at the table, digging at
its surface with her fingernail and a fork. (She is
dressed in dark clothing, short spiked hair.) She is
working her way through a package of chewing gum.
There are several empty styrofoam cups with cigarette
burns in front of her. A full ashtray. A box of half-eaten
take-out food. She gets up, stalks about, opening
drawers. She notices a piece of paper on a desk, reads it,
sticks it into her pocket. She goes to the back door
window and looks out. Finally, there is the sound of a
little engine outside. ROSE gets up and goes to back
door quickly.

ROSE:

(*calls out to someone*) It's me! Rose! Surprise! I'm here.
Yeah, it's me! I parked it out back in the garden. Hit
the tool shed and knocked over all your stupid rakes!

After a moment, ELIZABETH enters, leading a moped
laden down with shopping bags full of groceries. She is
flushed and cold from the outside. Late fifties, blonde
hair, a tired, wrecked face. Dressed in a heavy jacket,
wool cap, boots. Looks around at the mess, the peeled
oilcloth. She parks the moped in the middle of the
kitchen.

11

ELIZABETH:
How long have you been here?

ROSE:
Forever.

*After her initial burst of enthusiasm, ROSE is now quite
untouchable, walking about the room nervously,
lighting a cigarette, avoiding eye contact, stealing
nervous glances at ELIZABETH as she unloads her
moped.*

ROSE:
(*offhand*) You look like an old bag lady.

ELIZABETH:
You look like a malnourished bat.

*ROSE has a short nervous laugh. ELIZABETH starts
putting away groceries.*

ROSE:
There've been two wrong numbers since I've been
here. Someone wanting Nick and someone wanting
Edna. I hate it when that happens. Before I could
even tell them how stupid they were, they hung up.
Bloody rude. Then George called. Wanting to know
how you were. I lied and said you were doing fine.

ELIZABETH:
You haven't seen me in three months. Maybe I am
doing fine.

ROSE:
Your face doesn't look fine.

ELIZABETH:
(*rubs and pinches her face to tone it up*) I had a long
event-filled night.

ROSE:

Yeah? Me too. I had a dream about you pushing that stupid bike through a field of thistles in bloody bare feet. Then I dreamed George was being eaten up by cancer. It started in his left leg and progressed all over his body. There was a crowd at his door every morning waiting to hear what was going to give out next.

ELIZABETH:

It's nice that you think about your parents once in a while. How are the children?

ROSE:

All right.

ELIZABETH:

Just all right?

ROSE:

I guess so. Yeah.

ELIZABETH:

Tell me!

ROSE:

Jamie broke a tooth climbing over his sister in the bathtub.

ELIZABETH:

Oh no! Which one?

ROSE:

Claudia.

ELIZABETH:

Which tooth?

ROSE:

> The big jagged one at the front. Then she tickled
> him so hard he turned blue and his bellybutton
> popped out!

ELIZABETH:

> Poor Jelly Bean.

ROSE:

> And Janey kicked in the apartment window.

ELIZABETH:

> Why did she do that?

ROSE:

> She lost her key and couldn't get in after nursery.

ELIZABETH:

> Where was Mrs. Burke?

ROSE:

> She doesn't come anymore. Says she has a problem
> with her inner ear, has to stay in bed and put olive oil
> in it. Stupidest thing I've ever heard. The old bag
> never did like me.

ELIZABETH:

> She wasn't looking after you, Rose. She was looking
> after your children.

ROSE:

> Well not anymore.

ELIZABETH:

> Where are they now?

ROSE:

> When I gained consciousness this morning, I
> dumped them with their respective wimp-assed
> fathers.

ELIZABETH:

(*after a pause*) Well, it's good to see you.

ROSE:

Yeah?

ELIZABETH:

I was wondering how you were all doing.

ROSE:

Yeah?

ELIZABETH:

What do you mean "yeah?" Of course yeah. Come here and give me a hug, alien.

> *ELIZABETH steps in the path of her daughter. ROSE allows for a brief hug then pulls away.*

ROSE:

You smell like last night's Canadian Club.

           ❧   ❧   ❧

> *LOUISE, very agitated, with a notebook in hand. BETTY, aged 16.*

LOUISE:

I want to talk about the blueberries.

BETTY:

I knew this would happen.

LOUISE:

Did you?

BETTY:
We go through this every time you read my journal now.

LOUISE:
Because everything you write now is more fantastic than before! (*refers to notebook*) Like this. There are things I don't recognize.

BETTY:
Like what?

LOUISE:
Well ... we all go berrypicking, the whole family, including your father.

BETTY:
That happened, didn't it?

LOUISE:
Except he is a mystery man with no face.

BETTY:
It's an image ... a literary ...

LOUISE:
I know about literary images.

BETTY:
And that one doesn't do anything for you?

LOUISE:
No.

BETTY:
Not even when he stares past us at the dinner table like he's in a coma?

LOUISE:
No.

BETTY:

Or when he drifts off to sleep in his chair and his eyes roll way back until they ...

LOUISE:

No!

BETTY:

You used to think my journals were good reading.

LOUISE:

When you were describing fun things like visiting grandmother or bathing the dog.

BETTY:

Berrypicking was fun.

LOUISE:

But it's not really about berrypicking is it? It's about me. Out of the blue it suits you to quote me as saying "I felt totally alone during those hours of berry-picking, even though my entire family was within inches of me. I felt as alone as I could ever want to be." (*looks up from notebook*) I never said that. And then you announced to everyone in the kitchen that the *real* reason mother was in a bad mood after berrypicking was because no one had needed her for the whole afternoon. And you never said that. It's all fiction. It came out of the ether.

BETTY:

It came out of my heart.

LOUISE:

Which grows more out of control every day.

BETTY:

(*quietly*) That's not possible.

LOUISE:

Betty, I remember you saying lots of things. I remember, "Oh Mommy, I am getting blemishes all over my face and why am I so ugly. And, "Graham Spring smells like beans." But I don't remember that (*pointing to notebook*). And I don't believe you even thought that!

BETTY:

Well I did later.

LOUISE:

Well later doesn't count. And I don't believe you peed all over the blueberries. I think that later you wanted to think that you peed on the blueberries so that you'd sound like a little rebel but the fact was, my dear, you were one of the most meticulous, prissy, scheming little items to ever venture out of Rockcliffe.

Partial light up on GEORGE, his back to the audience. George laughs his wonderful, infectious laugh.

❧   ❧   ❧

ELIZABETH responds to this laugh, this memory.

ELIZABETH:

But I never strayed from …

ROSE:

From what? You never strayed from what? Hello !

ELIZABETH:

What?

ROSE:

Christ! (*grabs her bag of pills and pops a couple in her mouth*)

ELIZABETH:

Don't do that, Rose. You eat those things like Smarties. They just mess you up.

ROSE:

I'm already messed up.

ELIZABETH:

Is there something wrong? Have you got something on your mind?

ROSE:

Can't I just come and see you? I haven't seen you in ... how long did you say? Three months. You don't come around when you're in the city. You see the others and get potted with your rascally friends but you don't come to see me.

ELIZABETH:

You have no phone.

ROSE:

You could come by.

ELIZABETH:

The last time I came by there were strange messages tacked to the door. "Mojo was here. He wants his money tonight." And "Darlene finally came through." Do I want to know what that's about?

ROSE:

I was working as ... a messenger. That's all you have to know.

ELIZABETH:
> Oh Rose.

ROSE:
> But I quit.

ELIZABETH:
> What are you doing now?

ROSE:
> Selling flowers at Victoria Station. (*ELIZABETH starts to laugh*) Why is that funny?

ELIZABETH:
> I don't know. It just is. What do you wear?

ROSE:
> This. Stuff like this.

ELIZABETH:
> You're not exactly the epitome of romance.

ROSE:
> I do all right. And you're not exactly Jean Harlow anymore either. It's just a bloody job.

ELIZABETH:
> I guess so.

ROSE:
> (*continues to pace*) The kids miss you.

ELIZABETH:
> I miss them too.

ROSE:
> (*looks around resentfully*) You have a pretty funny way of showing it. Moving three hours away from them.

ELIZABETH:
> Don't say that.

ROSE:

Well that's what it seems like.

ELIZABETH:

Don't ever make them think that.

ROSE:

I don't. But don't you miss people out here?

ELIZABETH:

I see lots of people.

ROSE:

Like that toothless oaf on the tractor and the queer ducks in the smokeshop.

ELIZABETH:

And lots of others. Jeffrey comes out every Wednesday.

ROSE:

Good old Jeffrey.

ELIZABETH:

I have houseguests on the weekends. We have gourmet feasts, and wander about the garden between courses, reading poetry and sipping my berry wines. It's magnificent.

ROSE:

And what about when they all go home?

ELIZABETH:

What do you mean?

ROSE:

When you're by yourself. What do you do after they eat your food, drink your wine and go back to the city?

ELIZABETH:
I cook. I plant my garden, grow bulbs, review books.
I've even started to do some writing. I'm working on
a fun little thing about birds and beetles and well-
rotted compost.

ROSE:
Why don't you try science fiction or exposés on the
Royal Family?

ELIZABETH:
(*laughs*) I don't know a thing about the Royal Family.

ROSE:
So? Make it up. Use your imagination. That's what
writers *do*, isn't it? Look at ropey-necked old George,
imagining that he's 30 years old again.

Lights up on GEORGE.

GEORGE:
What a chaotic bitch she is. How did we manage to
create such a concentrated piece of chaos, Elizabeth?
Why do you put up with her?

ELIZABETH:
What are you doing here, Rose? It's too far for a
Sunday drive.

GEORGE:
(*leans back remembering*) When Rose came along, I
remember thinking ... that's four with the big
blonde, two with the thin one, maybe another one
down at Brighton with Melody Rourke, though it's
hard to say. I wasn't the only one sniffing around that
foxhole. Your genius, George, continues to rise up
and spread its bounty far and wide. Georgina by the
sea in America, Christopher and Sebastion under the

rubble of that awful basement flat on Pickwick. Then the two finally in my hallowed marriage bed on Regent. No doubt ever about their exact spot of origin. But then Rose. Rose. I've always thought of Rose as being the condensed anger of all women. And I was never quite certain when or where she took root. Was planted. Do you remember Elizabeth?

Lights on BETTY, in a pair of very short shorts. She admires herself in the mirror, while brushing out her thick mane of blonde hair.

ROSE:

Last night, I dreamt he was eaten alive by that stupid cross-eyed dog of his—Flaubert.

ELIZABETH:

Everything is stupid.

ROSE:

But Flaubert couldn't even stomach him and coughed him into a flowerbed in Kew Gardens where he came up as sort of a sickly deformed tulip.

ELIZABETH:

I think you make up your dreams when you are sitting on the M1.

ROSE:

What if I do?

ELIZABETH:

Do you need money?

ROSE:

No, I get by.

ELIZABETH:

Then why are you here, Rosie?

ROSE:
I came to comfort you.

ELIZABETH:
Comfort … for what?

ROSE:
You know, for what's happening.

ELIZABETH:
With Margaret Thatcher? The arms race? My hemorrhoids?

ROSE:
You know.

ELIZABETH:
No I don't. Tell me.

ROSE:
About George's wedding. I came to make sure you didn't crack up over it, fall to pieces.

ELIZABETH:
How thoughtful.

ROSE:
Apparently she's the same age as Georgina. The old goat is marrying his bloody oldest daughter.

ELIZABETH:
He is not marrying his daughter. She merely looks like his daughter.

ROSE:
Have you seen her?

ELIZABETH:
> I introduced them. She came to my going away party
> at the magazine. She was just starting off in layout.
> Straight from Devon, missed her family. I invited her
> over to meet the rascals at The Dog and Duck. Next
> thing I knew, George was buying her stout and
> reading her palm.

ROSE:
> You introduced them?

ELIZABETH:
> Yes, he probably never would have run into her on
> his own. He always avoided the magazine crowd like
> the plague. Yes, it was probably my doing, or her
> undoing.

ROSE:
> Unbloody believable.

ELIZABETH:
> I'm sure she'll have a pleasant enough go round with
> him.

ROSE:
> Lots of others have.

ELIZABETH:
> Yes.

ROSE:
> You don't mind?

ELIZABETH:
> Why should I?

ROSE:
Lots of others haven't married him.

❧　❧　❧

*GEORGE stands, nervous and impatient, in the living
room of BETTY's summerhouse, California. BETTY is
in the next room. Now 25. She stands in front of a
mirror, moves very close to the glass, speaks softly.*

BETTY:
Lovers are mindless they
higher than fears are hopes
lovers are those who kneel
lovers are those whose lips
smash unimagined sky
deeper than heaven is hell.

*GEORGE goes over to a large radio, flicks it on, twirls a
dial until he finds a channel with big band music,
turns it up loud.*

GEORGE:
So, do you think, Miss Smart, that minks enjoy
mating as much as their reputation would have us
believe?

BETTY:
Sorry! Can't hear you. Be right out though.

GEORGE:
That's all right. I've been sitting on a bus for five days
watching men in fields caressing cows. My head is full
of nonsense.

BETTY:

Still can't hear you.

GEORGE:

Obviously all North American women don't look as good as you.

BETTY:

Just make yourself at home.

GEORGE:

(*eyes liquor cabinet, goes over, pours himself brandy*)
Don't mind if I do.

> *BETTY enters. GEORGE smitten by her appearance, knocks back his brandy.*

BETTY:

Where is … is it Tess? Ness? Jess?

GEORGE:

It's Jess. She is putting things away in little drawers.

BETTY:

Do you have everything you need? Toothpaste, soap, towels. I don't think I put out enough towels. There are extra lightbulbs and flypaper in the cedar chest beside the woodstove.

GEORGE:

I think we'll manage.

BETTY:

I hope there's enough room down there … the bed is actually only three quarter.

GEORGE:

I'm sure it will be fine. Jess never moves during the night.

BETTY:

If you're cold, there are lots of extra blankets up here.

GEORGE:

I'm sure we won't be.

BETTY:

Just to be on the safe side ...

BETTY goes to a blanket chest and bends over, exposing her bare cheeks to a gaping GEORGE. She hauls out a couple of blankets and hands them to him.

BETTY:

You can take these down with you when you go to bed.

GEORGE:

Right.

BETTY:

You can work at this desk. The sun floods in all afternoon and the sea serenades you. At the end of the day, you can walk on the beach and buy fresh fish from the boats. There won't be anyone to bother you, no bills to pay, no air raid sirens, no worries, no aggravations ... Why are you looking at me like that?

GEORGE:

It's hard not to. You are a delight to the eye. Do you mind me asking why you're ...

BETTY:

Sponsoring you? I explained in my letter, didn't I? I saw some of your poems in a British journal. There was a picture. I liked your eyes, the humour in your face. I like the way you connect words together. No, I love it. I think you're a great poet.

GEORGE:

I am not that.

BETTY:

You are to me. I write as well. Millions of words. Lists, letters, journals, poems, diaries … anything that might get me closer to who I am. Am I making any sense?

GEORGE:

As much as I ever do.

BETTY:

And now I have a question for you. Why didn't you tell me you were married?

GEORGE:

(*laughs*) It never occurred to me.

BETTY:

You said you'd be arriving with your Olivetti, five pounds of your favourite typing paper, your bathing shoes, your bug bomb, your North American bird book, your D.H. Lawrence and a hunger for experience.

GEORGE:

I must have written that after coming straight from the pub.

BETTY:

Then you didn't mean it?

GEORGE:

Of course I did, but sometimes I'm given to hyperbole after a night at the pub.

BETTY:
Did you bring all of those things?

GEORGE:
Every single one of them. My D.H. Lawrence, my Olivetti, my virgin paper, my bathing shoes, my bug bomb, my North American bird book, my hunger ... and my wife. Do you mind?
They are standing very close.

BETTY:
(*after hungry pause*) I guess I've decided that I don't.
They kiss.

  ❧ ❧ ❧

Cottage, Suffolk.

ROSE:
If I were you, I'd kill him. After all you've been through, at least he could do right by you in your old age.

ELIZABETH:
I'm doing fine on my own. See? Look at my tulips, my herbs, my bachelor buttons ...

ROSE:
But you still think about it.

ELIZABETH:
I think about plants and nature and grandchildren and cute little human foibles I see around me.

ROSE:

And not George and the cute little human foible he
has taken up with? Not even once or twice while you
sit alone here in your cottage?

ELIZABETH:

If this is your idea of comfort …

ROSE:

Aren't you furious that he's marrying someone else
after you waited around for thirty years and raised all
his bloody children?

ELIZABETH:

You were mine too.

ROSE:

Doesn't it make you murderous to imagine that
horny old ram driving it into …

ELIZABETH:

And what if it does?

ROSE:

It does.

ELIZABETH:

I didn't say that.

ROSE:

It does.

ELIZABETH:

Rose, what is it that you want from me? You dumped
your babies with their "wimp-assed" fathers and
headed out here with your bag of drugs and your
fifteen coffees. Why? Obviously not to comfort me if
in fact you determined in your sensitive way that I
might need it. Or to bring the little angels for a visit.

You just came straight for me like a missile on target.
Why are you here? What right do you have to come
blasting in on me like this?

ROSE:

What right? I'm your chaotic daughter.

ELIZABETH:

Well what do you want from me?

ROSE:

How should I know? Maybe if I knew that, I wouldn't
be so chaotic. Did you ever know what you wanted?

୬ଈ   ୬ଈ   ୬ଈ

BETTY:

Yes! (*resounding climax to making love*)

> *GEORGE and BETTY are in darkness. Faint light shows*
> *them in bed. Laughter, fooling around, intimacy.*

I want you to tell me a story.

GEORGE:

All right. A story. A story about the great French
writer Flaubert, who doesn't have two pennies to rub
together, has ticks taking up residence in his ears,
and is whiling away his days in demented poverty in a
rat-infested garret on rue Rapin. Then suddenly, in
the space of a week, he has the incredible good
fortune of meeting an artistic well-mannered "clean"
handsome woman named Colette—the best France
has to offer; and then two nights later, an Egyptian
prostitute who smells like the sum total of all the
cooking in the Latin Quarter, has very bad teeth and

on top of that, is syphilitic. (*GEORGE breaks off, laughing*)

BETTY:

Why is that funny Barker?

GEORGE:

Old Flaubert is last seen sitting on a carton of week-old bread crusts, picking at his ears and trying to decide which one of these women he prefers. (*more laughter*)

BETTY:

And why is that so amusing?

GEORGE:

I don't know. It just is, don't you think? Not even a little?

BETTY:

No. I don't know what either of them would see in him.

GEORGE:

(*laughing even harder*) Maybe he had a very large vocabulary of erotica ... or maybe just a very large bird.

GEORGE playfully slaps some bare flesh, climbs out of bed, puts on his pants, looks at his watch.

BETTY:

Come back here. There's lots of time.

GEORGE:

I haven't written a decent line today. Nor an indecent one.

BETTY:

She won't be back for another two hours.

GEORGE:
Where did she go this morning?

BETTY:
The Enchanted Forest.

GEORGE:
Save my soul.

BETTY:
Come back.

GEORGE:
(*succumbs, drops back onto the bed and strokes her naked back*) You're a grasping, greedy thing. It's probably not your fault. It's your class, your beauty.

BETTY:
Tell me another story ... about George Barker.

GEORGE:
Then can I go back to work?

BETTY:
I'll see.

GEORGE:
Born the third son of a church organist and a Brixton refuse man. While we stayed home with mother and lit candles, my father collected garbage from the very best parts of town, until one afternoon, on Embassy Row, he expired while hoisting two hundred pounds of left-over liver paté.

BETTY:
(*laughing*) I don't believe you!

GEORGE:
Suit yourself. Life was for the most part very dreary until one day little Georgie stumbled on an

important realization. I was sitting on my stool in the garden and I noticed Rodney Taylor's mother through her bedroom window. She took off her dress, then her slip, then her great whopping brassiere and then proceeded to squeeze a wet sponge all over her large peachy tits. And from that moment on, I knew life need never be dreary again. I could escape into fantasy at the drop of a hat. Shortly after, I embarked on my own sexual mastery and finally I took to chronicling the whole delectable mess. And that's all there is. And here I am, even as I speak, engaging in all three.

GEORGE tries to extricate himself. BETTY pulls him back.

BETTY:
Why did you marry Jess?

GEORGE:
I thought she was like one of the saints in our church ... and that perhaps she could save me. At the very least, clean up after me.

BETTY:
And what did you think when you first met me?

GEORGE:
That you were a golden lion, circling a piece of meat.

BETTY growls hungrily.

Hungry, splendid, sensual ... and before we get carried away again ...

GEORGE tries to get up but BETTY pulls him back.

I have to work.

BETTY:

You don't.

GEORGE:

I do. I must.

BETTY:

Your writing is already perfect.

GEORGE:

That's not how it works.

BETTY:

It should be.

> *GEORGE finally frees himself, gets up and goes to the desk.*

Don't you want to hear my story?

GEORGE:

Not particularly. I'm sure it's just more upper class indulgence.

BETTY:

You're going to hear it anyway. (*gets up, throws on a shirt and starts circling about*) Born the second daughter of a slightly mad ex-debutante and an Ottawa patent lawyer. While we stayed home and crossed our little white socks at the ankles, my father practised law and my mother lifted silk stockings from department stores and gave them to homeless women in the park beside his office.

GEORGE:

You mean she nicked them? (*laughs*) I don't believe you!

BETTY:

Suit yourself. My life was for the most part hopelessly dreary. I was bored, cowardly, stupidly polite. I wrote volumes of mean-spirited diaries filled with minutia about nannies and the affronts of my sniffling sister; diaries which were regularly sent out and bound in leather. I didn't feel anything, I rarely thought anything and as such, my life was proceeding according to everyone's plan.

GEORGE:

My god, you're beautiful.

BETTY:

Until one day, I was sitting in my father's study staring dismally at my leather-bound collection, when I spied the corner of a flame-coloured book hidden behind *Tales of East Asia*. It was Lawrence's *Women in Love*, probably smuggled in by my poor mother. I devoured every word of it and for the first time, I felt something inside that can only be described as a hot coal burning.

GEORGE:

It's called sexual awakening.

BETTY:

It was *more* than just that. It wasn't just a feeling I had *there*. I felt there was a potential for my whole being to catch fire, that there were emotions inside me that could take me to the moon. Come here now. I want you. I want you here beside me so that I can worship you.

GEORGE doesn't budge from the desk.

GEORGE:
You can worship me from a distance.

࿊ ࿊ ࿊

Cottage, Suffolk. ELIZABETH is absorbed in her memories. ROSE pops some form of junk food into her mouth.

ROSE:
I've met someone. (*repeats loudly*) I've met a man, Mother. (*gains ELIZABETH's attention*)

I met him while I was selling flowers. He came out of the tube and stood beside the magazine kiosk for half an hour watching me. Then he came up and bought my whole bucket.

ELIZABETH:
Rose! How wonderfully romantic! What's his name?

ROSE:
William.

ELIZABETH:
Sweet William. Tell me about him.

ROSE:
He's not exactly sweet. More like Strange William. He's been in jail several times, has tattoos all over his arms. He wants to move in with me. Mrs. Burke didn't exactly take to him.

ELIZABETH:
Now it comes out.

ROSE:

He's a cut above the others, believe me. James likes him. He took them to the video parlour once and now they can't wait till he comes round. Little boys are so bloody easy to please.

ELIZABETH:

What about Jane?

ROSE:

She's scared of his tattoos.

ELIZABETH:

Maybe he should keep his shirt on when she's around.

ROSE:

It wouldn't matter if he wore a Bugs Bunny suit. Jane hasn't liked anyone since you looked after them. She's always asking when you're going to come back and make cheese dreams.

ELIZABETH:

Maybe you shouldn't rush into anything. Maybe you should get them used to the idea ... if you think this is what you want.

ROSE:

What I want ... by Rose Barker.

ELIZABETH:

Are you in love with him?

ROSE:

Now ask if I know what I'm doing.

ELIZABETH:

What does Strange William do?

ROSE:
Do?

ELIZABETH:
Why was he in jail?

ROSE:
A bunch of little things. What most people do but don't get caught at.

ELIZABETH:
Like what? Tax evasion, speeding, littering?

ROSE:
Little drug things.

ELIZABETH & ROSE:
(*unison*) Oh Rose!

ROSE:
Does that mean "Oh Rose, you're gonna get in trouble again?"

ELIZABETH:
I guess so. Yes.

ROSE:
How can you say that? You haven't even met him.

ELIZABETH:
Then you should have brought him out here with you today.

ROSE:
You wouldn't like him.

ELIZABETH:
Well then I'm glad you didn't.

ROSE:
Thanks a lot.

ELIZABETH:

You said I wouldn't like him! I took your word for it.
So what would have been the point?

ROSE:

The point?

ELIZABETH:

(*losing patience*) Rose, do you *want* me to like Strange
William?

ROSE:

(*miserably*) I don't know.

        ða   ða   ða

GEORGE is still seated at desk working.

GEORGE:

Don't pout. You said you were going to clean the
house.

BETTY:

Let's go swimming. Let's take a basket and pick
flowers down by ...

GEORGE:

(*cuts her off*) Let's be silent for fifteen minutes.

BETTY bends over, starts blowing smoke in his ear.

You haven't written one word since I arrived. Why is
that?

BETTY:

For that very reason! Because you're here! How can I
concentrate while you're with me?

41

GEORGE:
Writing requires discipline, concentration.

BETTY:
Don't chide me Barker!

GEORGE:
You're doing nothing.

BETTY:
I am doing research.

GEORGE:
(*laughs*) On what?

BETTY:
A book.

GEORGE:
A book about what?

BETTY:
Isn't it obvious? A book about love. You look almost frightened of me right now.

GEORGE:
I never pretended to be anything but a coward.

BETTY:
But you are more than a coward, George.

GEORGE:
What am I?

BETTY:
Something has happened in the last six weeks. The most miraculous thing of all.

GEORGE:
What is that, beautiful bitch?

BETTY:

We have been consumed by love. Melted together, ignited by love.

GEORGE:

Your metaphors are galloping.

BETTY:

We are in love George. (*grabs him*) Can't you feel it? It's inside us now.

GEORGE:

It sounds like a bacteria.

BETTY:

(*caressing him*) Oh shut up. Can you feel it?

GEORGE:

Oh god … I'm beginning to.

BETTY:

Can you feel it?

GEORGE:

(*succumbs*) I don't stand a chance.

❧   ❧   ❧

ROSE takes the letter out of her pocket, waves it around in front of ELIZABETH.

ROSE:

(*looking in direction of desk*) I found this among the ruins.

ELIZABETH:

What is it?

ROSE:

The letter from the Canadian university.

ELIZABETH:

You shouldn't be going through my mail.

ELIZABETH tries to retrieve the letter. ROSE moves away with it.

ROSE:

What does it mean when they say they want you to be writer-in-residence? Do they chain you to the heating pipes with your typewriter and let pimply students come down at lunch for a look? What a joke, eh? I wonder how they dredged up your name. It's sort of like the Chinese catching on to the Dave Clark Five ten years after we were using their records for hot-plates.

ELIZABETH:

What do you mean?

ROSE:

Some horny little Canadian professor probably found a copy of The Book in a library, blew the dust off, and discovered you! Thirty years after the critics here had spit you out and moved on to someone else.

ELIZABETH:

(*finally grabs letter, puts it back in desk*) They didn't spit me out. Anyway Rose, how would you know? You didn't exactly follow its progress. When you were twelve years old, you announced you would never read The Book, that you agreed with your grand-mother Louise, that it was a dead and sordidly regrettable thing. So dead, in fact, that you took the only copy you could find and buried it in the garden.

It was about that time that you stopped using any words with more than two syllables.

ROSE:

You're not thinking about going are you? Mother? Are you?

ELIZABETH:

It's kind of an amusing thought.

ROSE:

What is?

ELIZABETH:

To be taken seriously as a writer after so long.

ROSE:

More like pathetic. I bet it has to do with you being a Canadian. There's probably money to bring back funny old exiles. (*laughs*) I can see you arriving with your one book and your ten trillion unfinished poems and your knapsack full of Buckinghams and miniature liqueurs and yellowed reviews and that *look* on your face.

ELIZABETH:

What look?

ROSE:

I dunno. Sort of the way my kids look when I find one of them standing out in the rain. God, it's all so depressing.

ELIZABETH:

Why are you here, Rose?

ROSE:

I need to get away for a while. I need you to come and look after the kids.

ELIZABETH:

I thought Strange William was moving in with you.

ROSE:

That's after he goes on a trip. He wants me to go with him.

ELIZABETH:

A trip where? What for?

ROSE:

Amsterdam. Germany. Kind of a buying trip. He's starting up kind of a business. Do you need to know anything else? I was wondering if you'd come and make cheese dreams with the kids till I get back.

ELIZABETH:

And when will that be?

ROSE:

What?

ELIZABETH:

How long will you be away? A weekend. A week. How long?

ROSE:

Don't get so excited!

ELIZABETH:

Well, I need to know.

ROSE:

It's this writer thing, isn't it?

ELIZABETH:

(*very agitated*) The last time you went away for a weekend, I ended up looking after them for six months. I need to know. And the children need to know.

ROSE:
Why?

ELIZABETH:
Why? Because they need you! They love you!

ROSE:
They couldn't care less.

ELIZABETH:
Sometimes I wonder where your heart lives, Rose.

ROSE:
(*harsh*) Do you?

❦ ❦ ❦

LOUISE pacing, looking towards door.

LOUISE:
Am I going to meet him?

BETTY:
Not yet. Not until he comes out. He is writing. He can't be disturbed.

LOUISE:
It's like you're holding him prisoner.

BETTY:
He is writing. If he doesn't write, he gets very upset. His stomach backs up on him. He turns sort of purple. He's British. They're not very hardy.

LOUISE:
He is also a married man. You are acting like a … slut.

BETTY:

Mother, I'm not acting like anything. I am finally *being* myself!

LOUISE:

Then I am even more disgusted.

BETTY:

I have opened my heart to love, lust, passion, delight, jealousy... I'm not just dreaming about them or reading about them ... I am experiencing!

LOUISE:

Aren't you being selfish?

BETTY:

(*laughs happily*) Absolutely! But what's wrong with that? Haven't you ever wanted to be just ecstatically selfish? (*lets out a whoop of ecstatic delight*)

LOUISE:

At your age, I had a man in bed and he was my husband, not somebody else's, and there he remained each and every night for the next thirty years.

BETTY:

You sound proud of that.

LOUISE:

I am.

BETTY:

But how could you bear it? Think of what you've given up.

LOUISE:

Think of what I have.

GEORGE comes into the room. He doesn't see LOUISE at first and grabs BETTY lustily from behind.

GEORGE:
I heard your war cry.

LOUISE stiffens. GEORGE sees LOUISE and pulls away from BETTY, embarrassed. BETTY laughs, pulls him towards her mother.

BETTY:
Come, love, and meet ...

LOUISE:
I'm Betty's mother. And I know who you are.

They study each other.

LOUISE:
From Betty's letter, I expected you to be larger than life. But you're quite ordinary.

GEORGE:
Yes, quite. And from Betty's description, I expected you to be mad as a hatter, but you're stunningly sensible and if possible, even more beautiful than your daughter.

LOUISE:
I've been well cared for.

GEORGE:
I'm sure you have been.

BETTY:
(*jumping in*) Let's have a drink. Several drinks! We'll have a feast! This is a cause for celebration. My loved ones together at last. I'll go and get some champagne.

BETTY rushes off. LOUISE and GEORGE continue to study each other.

LOUISE:

Why are you doing this to my daughter?

GEORGE:

I think we are doing it to each other. I can't tell you other than that she has fixed me with her passion. I am like a poor bug that has been pinned to the wall.

LOUISE:

And yet it is she who will get hurt unbearably.

BETTY comes back with wine, glasses, and a bowl of cherries.

BETTY:

I bought these cherries this morning at the market but had no idea they were going to celebrate such a happy ... (*looks from one to the other*) What is this? A conspiracy?

LOUISE:

I have a train to catch.

BETTY:

Oh please don't go yet! Go tomorrow. Go the next day.

GEORGE:

(*interrupts*) Please don't leave on my account.

LOUISE:

That is exactly why I am leaving.

BETTY:

Mother!

LOUISE:
 I have to go.

 *BETTY follows her mother to the door and hugs her
 goodbye. BETTY turns back towards GEORGE, looking
 breathless and disappointed.*

BETTY:
 What?

 *GEORGE comes towards her and kisses her tenderly on
 the forehead.*

                ❧   ❧   ❧

 *Cottage, Suffolk. ELIZABETH is outside in her garden.
 ROSE is watching her. GEORGE, real or imagined, is
 there.*

ELIZABETH:
 Do you know why I love a garden, George? Because
 people who can't even appreciate the beauty of a
 sunset can list the contents of their gardens and they
 become poets: flowering stone, jacobinia, string of
 buttons, thyme, templebells, Swiss cheese plant,
 jonquil, wisteria, honeysuckle, baby tears, tulips,
 flame-of-the-woods. There is still passion in the
 garden. There are things that happen there which
 are heartbreaking. Plants are mad about creation.

GEORGE:

> Lying with, about, upon,
> Everything and everyone
> Every happy little wife
> Miscegenates once in a life ...

> *GEORGE is trying to complete the last lines of a poem, and is getting frustrated. BETTY is in the room.*

And every pardonable groom needs sometimes a change of womb because ... because although damnation may strike him ... although damnation may be at the end of it, the upshot, the rub, the long and bloody short of it, Christ, because although damnation may be ...

BETTY:

> ... society needs every ba-by.

> *GEORGE glares at her.*

BETTY:

Do you get it? Although damnation may be ... society needs every baby. You were having trouble so I thought I'd help. You're angry at me. I'm sorry. Pretend I'm just one of those birds chattering beyond the railing.

> *Cold silence.*

GEORGE:

You're disgusting. You are superficial, vacant, silly ...

BETTY:

I am none of those things.

GEORGE:

You are moody, selfish, spoiled, conceited and self-absorbed.

BETTY:

So are you!

GEORGE:

Since Jess went to San Francisco, there hasn't been a day complete without a crisis, some fiasco … a pipe broken, a toilet clogged, a pot burned, a bat loose in the house …

BETTY:

But we've read every word of *Sons and Lovers*, we've written a play, an epic passion poem! We've made love on the moss, in the ocean, on the beach, on the steps, in the daisies, the boat, on top of the typewriter …

GEORGE:

Have you made a list?

BETTY:

I don't need to. I remember them all!

GEORGE:

And you're oversexed!

BETTY:

(*laughs*) You were there too, George!

GEORGE:

What if she walked in and saw this mess?

BETTY:

What if she did? What does it matter? When she comes back, we're going to tell her about us anyway.

GEORGE:

About us? What about us? That we eat, sleep, forni-
cate ten times a day and even more on Sundays. That
I write the odd piece of nonsense while you bury us
higher and deeper in laddered stockings and dirty
dishes.

BETTY:

Jess will be all right.

GEORGE:

What do you know about people like Jess? With your
indecently beautiful easy privileged life?

BETTY:

People are all the same. They all need love.

GEORGE:

You say as you take away her husband.

BETTY:

There is another man for her somewhere. There isn't
for me. (*pause*) George, I'm going to sell some
mineral stocks and give Jess the money.

GEORGE:

Do you really think she'd accept it?

BETTY:

Why not? She's broke!

GEORGE:

Do you really think she'll be willing to sell what you
want to buy from her?

BETTY:

It's a gift, not a payment.

GEORGE:

You really believe that, don't you?

BETTY:
Yes!

> *GEORGE rubs his neck, discouraged. BETTY comes up behind him, begins massaging it. GEORGE closes his eyes. BETTY begins softly reciting a poem.*

I'll love you dear, I'll love you
till China and Africa meet
and the river jumps over the mountain
and the salmon sing in the street.
I'll love you till the ocean
is folded and hung up to dry
and the seven stars go squawking
like geese about the sky

GEORGE:
I'm sorry I said those things. I didn't mean them.

BETTY:
You're upset that I finished your thought.

GEORGE:
I'm upset that the thought was not worth finishing.
And that I am somehow … overwhelmed here.

BETTY:
By what, my love?

GEORGE:
I guess by you.

❧   ❧   ❧

Cottage, Suffolk.

ROSE:

> Writer-in-residence, eh? That's what you've always been sort of, haven't you, except you never wrote. You just resided. You wrote your one book and then after that, you were just "in residence". You might as well have been chained to the heating pipes.

ELIZABETH:

> You don't tiptoe around people's sensibilities do you? You just tear at them.

ROSE:

> I remember how you looked yearningly at books and smiled and talked and talked … you could have filled the Thames with all the words that came out of your mouth about writing. But you never wrote. I mean, George wrote. George made a big fucking deal out of writing. That's the way men are. But you couldn't seem to get the words out. You were always too tired or distracted or freaked out about one thing or another.

ELIZABETH:

> I was raising four children.

GEORGE:

> But why were you doing it?

ELIZABETH:

> What do you mean why? Who else was going to do it? It had to be done. Surely we at least agree on that, don't we?

ROSE:

> Nobody asked you to have four children. People must have thought you were quite a sight, walking around with your four little bastards.

ELIZABETH:
I'll look after the angels.

ROSE:
Pardon?

ELIZABETH:
I'll come into the city and take care of the children.

ROSE:
Don't change the subject!

ELIZABETH:
I thought that was the subject! I said if you need to get away, I'll come into the city and look after the children.

ROSE:
No! Don't sacrifice another thing for me!

ELIZABETH:
You said that's what you want. What do you want?

ROSE:
I want you to say something that's not wrapped up in surrender, and bravery and long suffering … something real.

ELIZABETH:
Rose, when you were ten years old, you told me that you felt there was sunshine inside you. You felt strong and clear-sighted.

ROSE:
I was never like that.

ELIZABETH:
You were for a while. What happened?

ROSE:

What happened? I remember you standing outside his house on Harrow Street in the rain with that stupid purple purse in your hand, the straps all twisted around your fingers.

ELIZABETH:

I remember him standing under our window serenading me till he had no voice left.

ROSE:

I remember all the pots with lids that never fit from you slamming them about.

ELIZABETH:

Why don't you remember the nice things? What about the time we went to Kew Gardens on the bus, the whole family. You arranged it all. And you made cookies and cakes and mushrooms stuffed with nutmeats. And we all dressed exactly the way you requested. I had to wear my yellow dress and flat shoes …

ROSE:

That's so you wouldn't trip over your high heels and spoil everything.

ELIZABETH:

And George wore his grey jacket which made him look like an undertaker.

ROSE:

It made him look like a judge.

ELIZABETH:

And you carried the lunchbasket and led the way singing "Onward! Christian Soldiers" which you learned god knows where. And everyone turned to watch 'cause you looked so sweet and determined marching along in your saddle shoes.

ROSE starts humming "Onward! Christian Soldiers" then as ELIZABETH talks, ROSE begins marching. ELIZABETH grabs a pot and bangs on it.

ELIZABETH:

And George beat time on a tobacco tin and Sebastion stuffed his trousers into his socks. And I turned my hat inside out and Christopher got so excited he wet his pants and we all got so silly that Georgina hid behind a hibiscus hedge and you went and yanked her out and told her that it didn't matter if we were making fools of ourselves, as long as we were all together.

ROSE stops singing, slows, stops, but ELIZABETH is still marching, banging on the pot.

ELIZABETH:

Come on Rose, Don't stop. This is fun. Why are you stopping?

ROSE:

Because in the morning, when we woke we weren't together, were we? He was gone. You were alone and staring at us like we were specimens from another planet. And all around you on the floor were crumpled half-filled sheets of paper and empty ... Why did you let that all happen? I hate my memories of you.

≥ *≥* *≥*

> *GEORGE is in the bedroom putting clothes in a suitcase.*

BETTY:

> (*entering, excited, her arms full of flowers, champagne and groceries*) I'm back! I've got champagne and shrimps and blossoms that smell so sweet they'll break your heart and strawberries and ... where are you, love?

> *BETTY enters the bedroom and sees GEORGE packing.*

> What are you doing?

GEORGE:

> Isn't it obvious? I'm leaving. I can't write here. I can't think here. There are no warts, no odours, no scars, no flaws, no weaknesses, no ugliness to draw upon. Instead I'm forced to look inside for material.

BETTY:

> Well that's good, isn't it?

> *BETTY comes towards him; GEORGE pushes her away.*

> It will be all right. The words will come again. I'll help. I won't play the phonograph loud or walk about naked. I'll make it better.

GEORGE:

> You can't.

BETTY:

> I can. I can do anything with my love.

GEORGE:

> No. That's where you're wrong.

BETTY:

> You belong to me, George.

GEORGE:

I'm married. I can't abandon my wife to live with you in this pretty sty.

BETTY:

I'm your true wife. I have the seed of our love growing inside me.

GEORGE:

What?

BETTY:

I am going to have your baby, George, and tonight we're going to celebrate.

GEORGE:

(*picks up a chair, lifts it high in the air and smashes it against the floor*) You planned this all along. You set about to trap me!

BETTY:

No.

GEORGE:

(*throwing things into the suitcase*) I don't want you. I don't want your child. Go back to your society life, parade your little indiscretion about in a pram, sit in cafés with your bored friends and tell titillating stories about your grimy British poet. I don't want anything more to do with you!

BETTY:

You don't mean that.

GEORGE:

I do.

BETTY:

You can't leave. I can't live without you. I'll go mad.

GEORGE:

You are already mad. And what is more, you're making me mad.

BETTY comes toward him.

Get away.

BETTY watches him for a while, then springs on him from the back with the full force of her rage, her love, her hate. She scratches his face. GEORGE fends her off. BETTY lunges at him again, biting, slapping, kicking. He throws her off and she lands in a heap of clothing on the bed, sobbing.

GEORGE:

Stop that. Please, please.

GEORGE puts his hands over his ears to block the sound, then slams shut his suitcase and leaves quickly.

                    ð   ð   ð

Cottage, Suffolk.

ROSE:

You get that dumb animal look on your face when you talk about love. I have to fight the urge to smash it in. You had it all. A lot more than me. You were beautiful, rich, sexy, smart. He knocked you up and left you—he used you and threw you out like an old safe. Why don't you just admit it?

ELIZABETH:

He left but I was still full of him, full of his inspiration.

ROSE:

You're full of bullshit.

ELIZABETH:

It was because of him that I wrote my book.

ROSE:

You don't hear! You never hear!

ELIZABETH:

Rose, if you want to go away I'll look after the little angels. I don't care about this writer thing. Rosie, you've got to let in the big feelings—keep your heart open. Why are you laughing?

ROSE:

Because I don't care about Strange William. Don't you see? I don't *care* about anything. The only big feeling I've ever had is anger at you. (*kicks over the moped*) Goddamned you! I'm dying inside and you tell me to let in the big feelings!

ELIZABETH:

Well what do you want me to do? Wallow about with you?

ROSE:

Yes! No! I don't know. Just do something!

ELIZABETH:

(*rage*)I have done enough. *Enough!*

    ROSE grabs her bag of drugs and storms out of the door.

End of Act One.

Act Two

ELIZABETH, alone in the cottage, looks out the window. Outside a car starts and stalls repeatedly. The car's loud radio comes on and off with each attempt to start the engine. The car door slams, the hood is thrown up, the odd curse is heard. We are aware that ROSE and her rage have moved outdoors. The car battery finally dies.

ELIZABETH:
Damn damn damn!

After a moment ROSE enters, stands, looks at her mother.

You should have turned the radio off.

ROSE:
I want out.

ELIZABETH:
(*quickly*) Well we could take your battery to the village and have it charged.

ROSE:
That's not what I meant. That's not what I'm talking about. I want out of this trap. I quit. I'm not going to do it anymore.

ELIZABETH:
(*frightened*) Do what?

ROSE:

If women were really honest, the world would be a different kind of place. I hate being a mother. I hate all the ick and the whines and the farts.

ELIZABETH:

Everyone feels that way once in a while ...

ROSE:

I hate every minute. And I don't want a man either. It just started to come clear to me out there as the battery died. I don't want any of it. I don't want a man or kids jumping all over me. I opened up my heart out there and the big feeling I got was freedom!

ELIZABETH:

Well it's not that simple. You can't just ...

ROSE:

I can do whatever I want, can't I? You did.

ELIZABETH:

I was different.

ROSE:

So was I. At least I always felt different. I had my O levels and greasy hair and Daryl breathing down my neck. I thought if we had a baby, I'd start to feel all that love bullshit you talked about. But it didn't happen. Daryl loved me all right, loved me to take his clothes to the launderette and squeeze the blackheads on his back. But by then it was too late to turn back. Claudia was on her way.

ELIZABETH:

Why didn't you stop then?

ROSE:

I was going to but I thought what was the bloody difference whether I had one or two? What else did I have to do? And one day, the sight of Peter's rollmops made me vomit and there were two of them tossing trucks at me. Then some stupid ad on the television made me think having a boy might be fun and no sooner had I thought that, the smell of Mickey's kippers made me sick and James came along. But it's not fun.

ELIZABETH:

Isn't it, Rose?

ROSE:

No. It's lonely and scary. And yet every woman I know has at least one little creature throwing trucks at her. What about you? Why did you have children?

ELIZABETH:

I love children.

ROSE:

(*sarcastic*) Oh? What did you *love* about them?

ELIZABETH:

I love their laughter. I love to have them swarming all over my lap. I loved that joyous feeling of getting everything going in the morning. Starting things up … being the creator of the day. Toasty warm babies, the smell of coffee …

ROSE:

You mean steamy windows and everyone fighting. I don't remember mornings being joyous. I remember you drinking jars of tomato juice.

ELIZABETH:
I remember little chuckles, tying shoes, the magic …

ROSE:
Living alone in a flat on Pickwick Street with colicky babies and bombs falling around you was magic?

ELIZABETH:
I remember feeling thankful for Georgina.

ROSE:
Thankful? To who? To George? When you were changing her diapers, swirling the dirty ones around in the toilet, were you thinking, "Thanks George?"

ELIZABETH:
"Nurses to their graves have gone and the prams go rolling on."

ROSE:
What?

ELIZABETH:
Just a verse.

ROSE:
Always a verse. Mother? Remember George? George is getting married today at three o'clock. Were you thinking, "Thanks George?"

❧   ❧   ❧

BETTY and baby in cramped flat in wartime London. Baby paraphernalia. Street noise. BETTY looks great, chattering away to baby in bassinet.

BETTY:

Let's go to the park, Georgie Porgie, see the ducks, buy some chestnuts, navigate our way around the clusters of horse turds and smelly old men. I'll spread out the blanket and put you down and you can gaze at the world through blades of grass and clover and pink mother toes. I used to think that London was such an ugly hopeless city but that was when I was a wretched little snot abroad with her nanny. Now that I have you to walk in the park, it is the most beautiful luscious city in all the world. Oh, I love you. And your father is going to love you too ... love you to pieces. (*A knock at the door; BETTY is startled, whispers*) He's come.

> *BETTY goes to the door and opens it to GEORGE. She moves out of the way, and he comes in tentatively, looking around.*

GEORGE:

Is there someone else here?

BETTY:

Yes, Georgina. I called her Georgina.

> *GEORGE looks at the baby bassinet and walks over to it. BETTY stands behind him, proudly.*

GEORGE:

Is she all right? Why is she so blotchy?

BETTY:

She's getting a tooth. Would you like to hold her?

> *GEORGE ignores the question and looks around at the flat.*

GEORGE:
What are you doing here?

BETTY:
What does it look like? I'm living here. I've finished my book and I'm looking for a publisher. I've got a typing job and a wonderful woman to look after Georgina who plays games like "round and round the garden" and "fiddledee faddledee foe … "

GEORGE:
(*cuts through gaiety, grabs her arm*) You've been leaving little notes for me in every pub in Nottinghill Gate. You've got to stop it!

BETTY:
Well I will now. Because I've found you, haven't I?

GEORGE:
Is this a game too? Like hide and seek? 'Cause if it is, I don't want to play. I am back where I belong. I sleep beside my wife and I am not disturbed. I teach empty verse to empty-headed students at the university. I drink with my friends and I write my poems.

BETTY:
Did you hear what I said, George? I finished my book. Would you like to read it?

GEORGE:
No.

BETTY:
Do you want to hold the baby?

GEORGE:
No.

BETTY:

Shall we read poetry? I've discovered a wonderful new Canadian called …

GEORGE:

(*interrupts*) I don't want to read it or hold it or talk about it. Nor do I want you to be here. Do you understand? I have recaptured my life. I am having an uncomplicated liaison with a ticket taker on the buses—a beautiful moon-faced girl who takes me up to her room after her shift. Then I make my way to the pub where I am probing the tormented mind of a reporter covering the war. My life is full.

BETTY:

It all sounds so exciting.

GEORGE:

It is. I couldn't be happier.

BETTY:

Neither could I. Be happier. That's why I've written the notes. I wanted you to know that. I wanted to thank you.

GEORGE:

Thank me?

BETTY:

For Georgina. For my experiences. For my book. I wanted you to know that I don't regret a thing.

GEORGE:

You don't?

BETTY:

No. And I'm glad everything has worked out. And I guess that's it.

GEORGE:

    I guess so.

    GEORGE hesitates, then reaches out and touches her hair.

    Except that your scent, your laughter, your wide blue eyes are the last things I remember as I fall asleep at night.

BETTY:

    Would you like to hold the baby?

GEORGE:

    First I would like to hold you.

              ❧   ❧   ❧

    Cottage, Suffolk.

ROSE:

    Let's have a party, Mom. Just you and me. I'd like to celebrate.

ELIZABETH:

    (*uneasy*) Celebrate what?

ROSE:

    My freedom. Freeing myself from kids, from Strange William—none of it really matters, does it? Just you and me matter. We're the only ones here. Have you got anything to drink? I've never known you to run out.

ELIZABETH:

    I've saved a bottle of gooseberry wine for a special occasion.

ROSE:

Well, let this be it. We haven't had fun together in a long time. You always say that things look better after a bout of riotous laughter and a little nip.

ELIZABETH:

Yes, I've always said that.

ROSE pushes ELIZABETH down on the couch beside her, opens the album and pulls out a picture.

Is that me?

ELIZABETH:

(*looks closely*) I had on my burgundy suit. No ... that's Christopher. (*ELIZABETH gets up*)

ROSE:

Where are you going?

(*ELIZABETH goes to cupboard, gets another bottle, opens it, fills her glass and downs it*) Get back here. Is that me with you?

ELIZABETH:

(*looks at picture*) I don't know who that is.

ROSE:

Did you colour your hair?

ELIZABETH:

You know I didn't, Rose. But you always ask me that.

ROSE:

Because it was so golden. So light. So beautiful. What did Louise call it?

ELIZABETH:

Angel hair.

ROSE:

This is fun, isn't it? (*turning pages*) There's George waving goodbye. I wonder where he was going that time. And there's George looking sullen, and there's you and George looking happy. And there's Jeffrey with his arm around you. Was he in love with you? Of course he was. Everyone was in love with you. (*ELIZABETH keeps drinking*) And there's Louise in her miles of mink. She always wore mink, didn't she? I remember sleeping on her mink coat one night she came to look after us when you had gone chasing after George. Is that me, Mom?

ELIZABETH:

(*looking at picture*) Yes, Rose, that's you.

ROSE:

How can you tell?

ELIZABETH:

You had a little corkscrew curl on the top of your head where the hair always grew faster.

ROSE:

Look! I still have it.

Puts ELIZABETH's hand on her head.

ELIZABETH:

So you do.

ROSE:

That's why I'm cutting it all the time. That's why it's always such a mess.

ELIZABETH:

Is that why?

73

ROSE:
Will you fix it for me?

ELIZABETH:
(*foggy*) Fix what?

ROSE:
My hair. Like you used to.

ELIZABETH tries to get the bottle again but ROSE stops her.

No!

ELIZABETH:
I don't remember how I did it, Rose.

ROSE:
That's 'cause you're always trying to forget. Here, I'll show you.

ELIZABETH gets to her feet unsteadily, stands behind ROSE, puts her hands in her hair. ROSE closes her eyes.

      ଌ   ଌ   ଌ

London, BETTY's flat. LOUISE sits at a table, dressed in a fur coat. She hears a sound, and jumps up nervously. BETTY enters; she is very pregnant. They haven't seen each other for a long time.

LOUISE:
I'm here for a war bond meeting. I let the sitter go early. I have a cab waiting.

BETTY:
Why?

LOUISE:

I wasn't sure what I'd find. Whether you'd be alone.

BETTY:

He may be over in a while. And then again, he may not.

LOUISE:

You smell like smoke and beer.

BETTY:

That's what happens when you go to the pub.

LOUISE:

And you're pregnant again.

BETTY:

That happened before I went to the pub.

LOUISE:

Don't be flippant!

BETTY:

I'm sorry but I feel exposed. If I had known you were coming I would have baked a cake. I would have polished up my silver. I would have … (*doesn't finish; sinks into chair in exhaustion*)

LOUISE:

Can I get you something?

(*BETTY shakes her head, closes her eyes. LOUISE gets up and stands behind her, instinctively starts rubbing BETTY's temples*) Your father sends his … love. Russell started law school last week. Your sister wrote and she loves her new house. Judith Helms got married in May. I brought you the newspaper clippings. It was called the wedding of the year except that two weeks later,

poor David got his diplomatic posting and it was for
Reykjavik instead of …

*BETTY grabs her mother's hands and holds on to them
tightly.*

BETTY:
Shhhh …

LOUISE:
What is it Betty?

BETTY:
Sometimes the walls press in so tightly I can barely
breathe.

LOUISE:
You can't stay here. Let's go home. Please let's just go
back to …

*BETTY pulls away from her, gets up and paces, lights a
cigarette.*

I've never seen you smoke.

BETTY:
You've never seen me do a lot of things. You've never
seen me haggling over a piece of lamb in the market
or queuing up for food stamps. No one tips his hat or
invites me for weekends in the country. I don't hear
the scuttlebutt from the embassies or the latest sex
scandal amongst the diplomats. But folks at least give
me a seat on the bus when I waddle on carrying my
one year-old. That's one good thing about being
down and out and up the stump in London.

LOUISE:
This is what this man has done to you.

BETTY:

No. I have done it all myself.

LOUISE:

Then you've gone crazy.

BETTY:

Mother, the world is crazy. Look around at what is happening. All I want is the love of one man. The love of one man.

LOUISE:

And do you have it?

BETTY:

(*doesn't answer*) There is something else that I want. I want to feel something big every day. Love, hate, lust, delight, despair ... Every day something big.

LOUISE:

Still so selfish.

(*BETTY laughs*) You have always followed your appetites.

BETTY:

And what have you followed?

LOUISE:

A belief in decorum, decency, order, certain standards of behaviour.

BETTY:

I have nothing against any of those things except that I can't for the life of me feel the heart in them. But let's not fight. It's good to see you. Stay for the night.

LOUISE:

(*gets up, prepares to leave*) I have a room at the Ritz.

BETTY:

Well stay for a while. He'll be here soon maybe. Stay and see him again.

LOUISE:

I'd rather see the Fuhrer. (*as she stands at the door*) Are you still writing?

BETTY:

(*hesitates*) I don't have the time now.

LOUISE:

I'm sorry to hear that. Although it never quite hit the mark, I thought you were at least trying to be honest.

> *BETTY stares rather longingly at her mother, not wanting her to leave, then gives her an awkward pregnant hug. LOUISE leaves. BETTY stands, looking after her. GEORGE enters.*

GEORGE:

(*looks around*) I smell her perfume. She comes and goes like the morning fog.

BETTY:

I want to get married.

GEORGE:

I see your mother's hand at work.

BETTY:

You see nothing. You appreciate nothing. I am not allowed to feel jealous that you sleep in another woman's arms, that you're not with me when your babies are born. My life is monstrous.

GEORGE:

Everything is a superlative.

BETTY:

Yes!

GEORGE:

You're upset because you're pregnant.

BETTY:

I'm upset because I don't want to share you any longer. I want it all. Everything.

GEORGE:

You said you wanted nothing.

BETTY:

I lied.

GEORGE:

I thought you did.

> *An air raid siren starts up and becomes all present. The baby cries.*

Oh Christ!

> *A bomb drops nearby. The lights go out. GEORGE grabs the baby and BETTY's hand and he hits the floor. BETTY remains standing.*

This is going to be a bad one.

BETTY:

Marry me.

GEORGE:

We are married. In spirit.

BETTY:

Then let the big one drop right now on top of us all. Georgina and you and I and the yet-to-be-born one ... melt us together for all time. Oh how sweet!

*Another bomb, even closer, flashes light through the
windows. Then darkness returns.*

GEORGE:

This may be it.

BETTY:

Well then let's put words to it. I, Elizabeth, student of
love, marry you George, and will love you with my
whole soul and with no reservations, and if you will
reciprocate, I will love you forever and forgive you
your blackest sins. Now you say it, George. Say it.
(*Another bomb, closer*)

GEORGE:

(*voice wavering*) I, George, marry you Elizabeth, and
will love you to the very depths of my blackened
poetic soul to the depths of your sweet radiant soul.

BETTY:

And with no reservations.

GEORGE:

And with no reservations.

BETTY:

Now we will kiss.

> *Another bomb drops. The baby cries. GEORGE and
> BETTY kiss. The bomb hits, this time farther away.*

(*babbling*) Georgina? Is she all right? Are you all
right? I'm all right. And we'll be together now.
Forever in spirit ... the only true way ...

GEORGE:

(*delighted to still be alive, pulls her back down, laughing*)
Oh hush, you little magpie!

Suffolk, Cottage. ROSE goes to a bookshelf and takes out a book.

ROSE:

I think it's time we read The Book. That would be fun, wouldn't it?

ELIZABETH:

Why now, Rose?

ROSE:

Because I don't care about it anymore. I'm freeing myself from all this sordid regrettable ancient history in the same way that George is freeing himself. Out with the old, in with the new.

ELIZABETH:

Give that to me.

ROSE:

(*opens the book*) "I am standing on a corner in Monterey waiting for the bus to come in … "

ELIZABETH:

Give it to me.

ROSE:

(*continues louder*) " … and all the muscles of my will are holding my terror to face the moment I most desire."

ELIZABETH comes across the room and tries to grab book out of ROSE's hand. ROSE holds it high above her head.

ROSE:

I thought you wanted me to read it. I thought you wanted everyone to read your Book.

ELIZABETH:

I want you out of my house.

ROSE:

How inhospitable. And you such a party girl. Let's go on. (*turns to another page*) "There are no minor facts in life, there is only one tremendous one." Which one is that, Mom? Betrayal?

ELIZABETH grabs for the book again, almost falling over.

We're having fun, aren't we? I'm trying to be more like you. Not so serious. More of a free spirit. I'm doing my best. And what about you? Why do you look so ...

ELIZABETH:

I am the happiest woman in the world.

ROSE:

"The page is as white as my face after a night of weeping. It is as sterile as my devastated mind." Are those the words of the happiest woman in the world?

ELIZABETH:

I could have married him. I did marry him.

ROSE:

(*shouts*) "Lay aside the weapons, love, for the battles are all lost."

ELIZABETH:

Get out of my house!

ROSE:

Why do you want me to leave?

ELIZABETH:

Because you are a misery. Because you mock everything that is beautiful.

ROSE:

No! I am looking for something that is beautiful.

ELIZABETH:

Our love was beautiful.

ROSE:

Was it? I remember Jeffrey coming by with his stupid bag of gumdrops and news of George. He'd say: Give up on him, Betty. He treats his dog Flaubert better than he treats you. He's a stray, Betty. He is sleeping with all his students, male and female.

ELIZABETH:

(*almost in trance*) My love is an artist. He needs experience. He hungers for the anguish that it brings. As do I.

ROSE:

Your lover used you, Mother. Just like everyone used you. Because you were so usable and reusable and pathetically innocent and saintlike ...

ELIZABETH:

I was no saint. I was no innocent! (*lunges for the book. ROSE drops it on the floor in front of her.*)

ROSE:

Take the book. I don't need it. I know it off by heart! Every pitiful word of it.

૨૦ ૨૦ ૨૦

*Book launch. GEORGE leafs through The Book. BETTY
approaches, surprised to see him.*

GEORGE:

Behold a woman in her most maternal and literary
glory. See how the body sags, the gait becomes
awkward, comical, in the same way that in her book,
the images are leaden, her euphemisms flowery, her
vision clouded by too much maternal milk.

BETTY:

(*devastated*) You said you loved the book.

GEORGE:

I can change my mind can't I? I am, after all, a great
poet. Isn't that what you've always said? Isn't that why
you went out and acquired me? What a pretty new
gown. Did you buy it specially for your book
launching?

BETTY:

It is a present from Jeffrey.

GEORGE:

A present from Jeffrey. How nice. How thoughtful.
How different from me. (*reaches out and pats her
stomach*) And how is our baby, little Mother?

BETTY:

(*pulls away*) It is my baby.

GEORGE:

Was it an immaculate conception? (*takes out a pen,
begins writing in the book*)

BETTY:
What are you doing?

GEORGE:
Autographing it. It seems only right. I was the one who provided you with your voice. I was the raw material. But now it seems you've been flittering off to my most harmless of friends in order to …

BETTY:
Flittering? I have two children and one on the way!

GEORGE:
(*roars*) And they are beautiful children! And they are mine!

BETTY:
But you are not there! You don't want me and yet you won't let anyone else have me!

GEORGE:
Do you want anyone else? What is it that you want? My shoes obediently at the door by five o'clock. A newspaper in front of your face in the morning, grunts from behind it indicating life. A perfunctory roll in the hay once a fortnight.

BETTY:
That would be more than I get now.

GEORGE:
Perhaps you should post your rates by the bed. A new dress here, a necklace there, Royal Doulton dishes for a good long stretch of it … the price of a lifetime. You're as much of a high class whore as your mother!

BETTY slaps his face.

BETTY:

You're jealous that I've finally got some attention for my words.

GEORGE:

No! I take that back! You are even worse than your mother. Your mother didn't spread her legs for the sake of the arts!

BETTY:

And you didn't? In your never-ending quest for experience, you have upended half the women in London.

GEORGE:

And I've loved every minute of it!

BETTY:

You are jealous that I can write and create babies.

GEORGE:

You're a cow!

BETTY:

You can't bear not being the centre of attention even for the few tormented hours it takes to bring them into the world.

GEORGE:

It gives me time out from the nagging!

BETTY:

And so you go out in search of every young literary groupie who will ease your terror of wrinkles and a sagging bottom and dried-up, tired-out, over-worked phrases!

BETTY's comments have hit home. GEORGE turns to leave.

࿊   ࿊   ࿊

LOUISE approaches with book in hand. BETTY, distressed, is still looking after GEORGE.

LOUISE:
I've read the book, Betty. Your book of love.

BETTY:
What do you think?

LOUISE:
I hate it. But that's not why I'm here. I want to take the children back with me to Canada.

BETTY:
Don't be absurd! Why on earth would you do that?

LOUISE:
Because I don't feel that you're fit to raise them. Hear me out! Living in basements, one month here, one month there, never enough heat or food, never any order or security ...

BETTY:
(*interrupting*) I don't care about those things. They don't matter.

LOUISE:
They are fundamental! But you can't understand that. You have never recognized ... the limitations.

BETTY:
And what are they Mother? Tell me again, maybe I'll understand them now.

LOUISE:

You are a woman, Betty, perhaps beautiful, but a woman nonetheless, and now rendered helpless by children in a man's world.

BETTY:

Not helpless. If anything, more powerful.

LOUISE:

But only if you accept those limitations and work with them. That's all I've ever asked you to do. Accept order, respectability, compassion …

BETTY:

But it's all a facade.

LOUISE:

And what if it is? It breeds optimism for all those around you and you'll be cherished and cared for and what's more, your children will be cared for.

BETTY:

But what about passion? Your desire for ecstasy? What about your pitiful volume of *Women in Love* hidden away behind *Tales of East Asia*?

LOUISE:

What about them? They were all just part of it.

BETTY:

But it is everything to me.

LOUISE:

And what will it be for your children? What kind of life are you giving them? Showing them love in fits and starts, crowding them out with your own torrents of emotions, your tumultuous comings and goings. You've got to leave some space for flowers to grow.

ROSE:

I want out. (*goes to the table, grabs her plastic bag of pills and starts stuffing them into her mouth*)

ELIZABETH:

(*horror*) Stop that!

ELIZABETH lunges at ROSE, knocks the bag away, scattering pills all over the floor. The two of them go down on their hands and knees scrambling to collect them.

ROSE:

Don't Stop me! I want out! Let me out!

ELIZABETH:

No!

ELIZABETH puts her hand in ROSE's mouth and starts pulling the pills out.

ROSE:

I came for help, but there is none. You were just another poor victim like the rest of us. Except you had your stupid little book to defend you. And now it's three-thirty and he's getting married and you're stuck here with your loser of a daughter, getting drunk for the nine millionth time. Just another red-eyed victim.

ELIZABETH slaps ROSE across the face. ROSE hauls off and hits her back.

ELIZABETH:

I was no victim! I was an explorer!

ROSE:

Then you lost your way.

ELIZABETH:

Yes I did, thousands of times! But I found it again.

ROSE:

And where did it get you?

ELIZABETH:

Where does anything get you, you silly bitch. Where does a beautiful day get you? I got a magnificent man.

ROSE:

Who's marrying someone else today.

ELIZABETH:

It got me four children.

ROSE:

Who complain behind your back and use you.

ELIZABETH:

I wrote a book.

ROSE:

Thirty years ago and nothing since. It doesn't add up.

ELIZABETH:

It's a life, not a balance sheet. What do you want me to say? That it was a disaster?

ROSE:

It was, wasn't it? And hard.

ELIZABETH:

Yes, it was hard. I wanted to be a lover and a writer and a mother and I botched them all up. Is that what you want to hear? Well, there it is. My life has been a snarl of exotic excuses, half-finished conversations, bottles, poems, cigarettes, seductions ... and sometimes, in moments of dreaded solitude, I am filled with disgust. But at least I tried, Rose. I did try. And I fell in love.

ROSE:
With what?

ELIZABETH:
With everything. With a man, with a fantasy, with words, and with that love, I felt I could do anything.

ROSE:
You deluded yourself. That's all any of us do.

ELIZABETH:
No!

ROSE:
Yes!

ELIZABETH:
No! I got exactly what I wanted. I loved being buried alive by my love. I needed to be needed. And he still needs me, oh yes, and I need him ... like the ground needs rain, I need him.

ROSE:
And what about me? Did you ever need me? Did you ever love me?

London. BETTY in flat. There is a knock at the door.
She looks at the door, but doesn't move. Another knock.
Finally she goes to the door and opens it to GEORGE.
He comes in and looks around, disoriented.

GEORGE:

This place is all right. At least it's above ground.

BETTY:

I'm making more money now. I have a new job.

GEORGE:

Where are the children?

BETTY:

It's 2:00 A.M., George. Where do you think? Why have you come here?

GEORGE:

I'm not sure.

BETTY:

(*studies him*) Is it your new book? I read the reviews. They're nonsense of course.

GEORGE:

Are they? You don't have to be charitable. I wasn't with yours. What's the new job?

BETTY:

I write copy for lipstick ads.

GEORGE:

Fiery, hungry, pouty, unquenchable, fleshy, sticky, bloody, sore …

BETTY:

You called and said you wanted to talk. Why are you here, George?

GEORGE:

They called me a minor poet. I don't know where I fit anymore. The world is a cold, unfeeling place. The nomadic visionaries are being replaced by earth-movers and builders and architects. No one cares about romance anymore.

BETTY:

I do.

GEORGE:

Yes. You do.

BETTY:

Where have you been?

GEORGE:

With a springy young thing from Keswick for the last ... I don't know ... week, month, year ... has it been a year? Surely not. (*seems tired*) She's taught me all about weaving cloth and jarring fruit. A regular little cottage industry she is. She has these enormous jugs in which she stores her jams and jellies. And she finds me delightful. How is it that you remain so disgustingly beautiful? I used to think you were just a glittering empty package that I could throw away like Americans toss away soda pop bottles. But you weren't. And you scared me to death. I've deceived you. I've been a coward. You say I created love for you, but I have also murdered it. I don't have the strength to love the way you do. I do live in terror of wrinkles and a sagging bottom and dried-up, tired-out phrases. I flee from them. I flee from anyone who names them, calls them what they are. I don't think I'll ever change.

BETTY:

I know.

GEORGE:

But I love you, Elizabeth. You are a glory to the world. Do you still want me?

Pause.

BETTY:

I'll probably get pregnant.

BETTY contemplates this, then comes over to him, slowly begins undressing him, unbuttoning his shirt, kissing his naked chest. GEORGE closes his eyes.

⁂

ELIZABETH:

I heard about Louise's death while I was standing in the post office on Water Street. There was a telegram. All of you children were there, rushing around me in coloured circles as if I were a maypole. I loved her. And I love you, Rose. I chose you. But she was right. I didn't take enough care. I didn't leave enough space for flowers to grow. I'm sorry. But I did try. And you'll have to try too.

ROSE:

I don't know how.

ELIZABETH:

You'll have to find out. You'll have to learn. I can't do that for you.

ROSE:

What are we going to do now?

ELIZABETH:

I'm going to go to that Canadian university and be their writer-in-residence. Maybe if they chain me to the heating pipes, I'll finally be able to finish my poems.

And you, Rosie?

ROSE and ELIZABETH look at each other for a long while.

The End